CONSTITUTION

Philipp Ursus Krautschneider

The subjective constitution

and its rationale

ISBN: 9798293538836

Independently published

Contact the author:

pino.sparks587@gmail.com

In memory of my mother

List of Contents

Introduction

There are those for whom reading and writing are of little importance. But I had decided to explore the human spirit in grounding depth and report on my conclusions. The generalisation principle – something I encountered in lessons in the first year of my secondary schooling – formed the starting point of my considerations. It was apparent to me that my teacher, as he described the generalisation principle, appeared to be anything but comfortable. This made me think that something must be missing, that the generalisation principle, despite being an evidently correct doctrine, could only represent one facet of reality as a whole. From that point on, I knew what I had to do.

At school, I was considered a bit of an overachiever with particularly skills in mathematics and physics. After school, I went on to study law because that was the area of particular interest to Immanuel Kant. I have, I believe, considerable capacity for empathy and using this in all my friendships and acquaintances with persons from various social strata, I attempted to construct the most accurate concept I could of intersubjective reality. I also practiced various sports in order to keep myself physically fit.

Of course, not everything ran according to plan. You have to break eggs to make an omelette. And so, during this processing stage, I was diagnosed with a psychiatric disorder and events occurred that, although they were essentially harmless, were the result of unaccountable behaviour on my part. Even in my career as a lawyer there was much that was not as perfect as it could be.

Finally, and after 25 years, I managed to find an adequate way of describing the principle of the basic norm ("Grundnorm") as related to law. But that wasn't enough. I was still not intellectually able to find a logical correlation in which to place the basic norm. So I decided to start blogging and invited everyone I knew to visit my website. I tried to put my highly abstract ideas into concrete form in a doctoral dissertation written for the University of Vienna but the attempt failed – my style was not up to the task. But then, on 7 January 2019 – almost 30 years after I had first had the idea, everything suddenly came together. The concept of The Subjective Constitution was born.

Since managing to define this concept and put it down in

writing, my life has taken a turn for the better. I have ceased to worry about my diagnosis. I can now express hopes and see them come to fruition while always striving to present a shining example of myself to the world. In the meantime, I have come to realise just how privileged I am. I was born in Austria, in Europe, and live here, I am a member of a well-to-do class, I was able to study and so on.

I hope that this work will serve to some extent as a justification of my privileges and that my outline here of my notion of the subjective constitution will prove to be of considerable value. I believe that in the more advanced countries of the world, it could even initiate a new Enlightenment, awakening interest in the subject and helping others to learn to understand themselves better, to better orientate themselves in general and thus discover the joy of living.

If some of the language I've used here is difficult to understand, this is because I've had to deal with my topic from a very abstract point of view and also, because it was important to me to avoid misinterpretations and misunderstandings. But if considered attentively and perhaps with a little research, I think my readers will find that my argument is both consistent and considered. The underlying concept, that of the constitution from a subjective viewpoint, is covered in chapter 1 and this, I hope will prove to be perfectly intelligible on its own. Hence, assuming that a reader does not require or wish for any further explanation, they can put this book aside after a mere 5 minutes reading time.

1. The Subjective Constitution

We all know the constitution. Usually, we describe our emotional status or the national constitutional with this phrase, upon which the national legal order is stated. I will try here to abstractly define the individual Subjective Constitution within the legal sense. The possibility of such a definition is evident with the following explanations:

The human constitution is always located between two extreme points, but only closer examination shows there are no fewer than five extreme points. Each of these points is expressed by a constitutional norm, which should be interpreted with the same care and originalism as of the national constitution. All individual constitutional norms are understood as a priori norms, while they are (partly) linked.

If simply two extreme points are assumed, so they are

described on the one hand through the basic norm of every mammal: „Someone else ought to feed me." and on the other hand through Immanuel Kants principle of generalisation: „Act only according to that maxim whereby you can at the same time will that it should become a universal law." These extreme points are linked in a way, that the basic norm as the first constitutional norm is to be subsumed under the criterion „universal law" of the principle of generalisation, according to a (more or less disciplined) hierarchy of the legal system at least as higher ranking law, particularly as constitutional law. It is essential that the basic norm only acts upon other persons than the subject of the constitution while the principle of generalisation only acts upon the subject itself, so that between these both norms there can never emerge an immanent contradiction.

If a closer look at the constitution is wanted, the extreme points can be further differentiated in the following relevant ways: With regard to the principle of generalisation, there is a difference, if the „universal law" is understood within legal meaning, ruling human behavior, or within natural principles describing only the reaction of things under certain circumstances. The basic norm on the other side can be organized precisely into three basic norms narrower sense, each of which has different consequences for the constitutional subject. The first basic norm narrower sense is spelled: „Someone else (female) ought to feed me." the second basic norm in this sense: „Something ought to nourish me." and the third: „Someone else (male) ought to feed me." The reasons for making a difference between female and male agents are the constantly different claims which are risen in life and also circumstances, that in general all humans are born from a woman, and this concerning basic norm therefore demands a certain timely precedence.

In sum the Subjective Constitution is nominated, with regard to the time of their first experiences in the following order:

Art. 1. „Someone else (female) ought to feed me."

Art. 2. „Act only according to that maxim whereby you can at the same time will that it should become a universal law (legal meaning)."

Art. 3. „Something ought to nourish me."

Art. 4. „Act only according to that maxim whereby you can at the same time will that it should become a universal law (natural principle)."

Art. 5. „Someone else (male) ought to feed me."

2. Fundamental considerations of the "Grundnorm" or basic norm

We humans are creatures that thrive on feel. The phrase: "Someone else ought to feed me" may not be the ideal way of expressing this concept but does take account of nearly all of the corresponding underlying aspect of feels. But the basic norm (as we'll call it in the following) attempts to bypass definition of the corresponding feels per se by means of artificial exaggeration. It is only in this way that an appropriate consideration and systematic analysis of the basic norm become possible.

But it is feel that gives meaning to the basic norm. Hence, the basic norm must always be viewed in the light of the specific feel (e.g. what is being "fed", what is actually happening and – in particular – what is the related feels). Originally, the concepts of the basic norm and feel must have evolved simultaneously but through our experience we tend to believe that the basic norm should be given priority over the relevant feels. Hence, a basic norm always "predates" the feels to which it refers.

The basic norm deals with reflexive needs. These needs can be expressed, for example in the first, second or third person "I ought to feed myself", "You ought to feed me" or "He/she/it ought to feed me". The basic norm does not appear to be directly relevant to the fourth person (viz. "Someone else ought to feed me") for which reason this person is used to provide an abstract paraphrase and preceptive breakdown of the basic norm. In the case of the fifth person, however (viz. "God ought to feed me"), the basic norm does appear relevant.

It is to be assumed that the need expressed in the first person ("I ought to feed myself") cannot develop in evolutionary terms before the emergence of the human "I". On the contrary, it is assumable, the "I" forms only through contact with other persons (particularly the second and third persons) on which fundament the basic norm gradually consolidates. This process actually occurs mainly in connection with individual, personal experiences and the feels and sensations felt by a small child in the relationship with those persons to whom it originally relates most closely. For this reason, ethical demands – i.e. demands an individual places on oneself – are to a large extent determined by how a human person is brought up as child.

Because of this and also in view of the concept of originalism, I consider my doctrine in the subjective constitution that the basic norm is directed only at other people rather than the "constitutional" subject themselves to be particularly important. Although the obligation "I ought to feed myself" can be derived from the basic norm, this would be – depending on corresponding feels – simply a subjective law but not a subjective constitutional law. It should also be borne in mind that the development of the "I" and the development of first-person needs continue after childhood and positive experiences in this connection are also necessary.

At the same time, the impact of the basic norm can be made to vary. Depending on this impact and the nature of the specific feels (sensations), the interpretation of the basic norm can be downgraded to the more easy-going {at special opportunities}: "It would be really, really nice if someone else were {as opportune as} to feed me", or made more forceful {and urgent} − "Someone else better feed me {at once}, otherwise..." All these meanings can be covered by use of the verb "ought". Hence, the consequences of compliance or non-compliance with the basic norm − success and failure − must be quite differently evaluated.

3. The sovereign will

As I have already pointed out in my discussion of the basic norm, it is principally feels and sensations that give this norm their sense and purpose (see Chapter 2). We learned through experience to prioritise this norm over sensations; and by means of compliance with the norm, can give our sensations full rein.

But **not every sensation is pleasant.** Because we experience unpleasant sensations we require norms that help us avoid such disagreeable sensations or, to put it another way, that make it possible for us to live without encountering these sensations. Humans need to learn these norms and how to apply them to survive.

For the purpose of simple differentiation, I shall call these norms "negative norms" while the norms focussed directly on sensations I shall call "positive norms". While sensations are in principle the direct fulfilment of positive norms, this is not the case with negative norms – this means that **negative norms are more continuedly existent.**

The sovereign will of an individual person expresses itself in such a concrete positive norm, that derived from the experiences made by that individual person but taking into account all negative norms in such a way, that their sense and purpose does not impact adversely on the desired sensation.

Although I am here writing of the norm system of an individual, the following quotation from Montesquieu's *Spirit of the Laws, Book XI, section 3* I think is relevant to my argument: *"In what Liberty consists. It is true that in democracies the people seem to act as they please; but political liberty does not consist in an unlimited freedom. In governments, that is, in societies directed by laws, liberty can consist only in the power of doing what we ought to will, and in not being constrained to do what we ought not to will. We must have continually present to our minds the difference between independence and liberty. Liberty is a right of doing whatever the laws permit. [...]"*

Considering this on the metalevel, it is apparent that **it is individual experience that essentially leads to the formation of the sovereign will.** On the one hand, this occurs by means of extension of the period of validity of positive norms or, in other words, by means of the experience-based expansion of the planning horizon. On the other hand, there can be a concentration of avoidance strategies in the form of negative norms or, to put this another way, this can occur by means of an experience-based increase in inhibition. Whether the one or the other occurs depends mainly on whether the original sensation was felt to be pleasant or unpleasant.

4. Democracy

In view of the concept of the sovereign will of the individual Thomas Hobbes concluded in his *Leviathan* that because humans strive for power the "**war of all against all**" (bellum omnia contra omnes) would be possible in human existence in a state of nature (see Chapter 3). We know that negative norms represent avoidance strategies and that if an individual is threatened by another individual these strategies can thus be employed for the purposes of defence (or even prevention). In the light of Hobbes' thought experiment above, this could be interpreted as a form of "war".

In reality, however, everyone has a birth mother and it is usually the case that this mother and/or the family educate and instil moderation on the part of the child. It is the **way that this moderation** and its innumerable facets and variants are imbued in a growing child that determine whether that child will grow up to become a principled individual who will be able, under circumstances, to dispense with the defence strategies available to them – particularly in the form of physical violence against others – for the common good.

This ability of individuals to forgo the use of physical force is a major element of what constitutes a state, the community of its citizens. In this context, it is standard practice to speak of the "**social contract**" (Jean-Jacques Rousseau). In an organised state, only certain organs of that state are authorised to exercise force (**state monopoly on force**), and in a developed state, the exercise of force is allowed only under specific legally defined conditions.

The **most developed form of government is democracy**. This is because in a democracy, it is undisputed that laws – in the objective sense – have their origin in the population of citizens. Actually, objective laws always evolve from what are (initially subjective) negative norms (see Chapter 3).

The prerequisite for and main characteristic of a democracy is the moderation exercised by its citizens. There can and, in fact, must be certain extreme positions within any democracy but **the middle ground stays always practicable and of heavy importance.** If the extremes once begin to predominate in a democracy, the state is threatened with unrest, such as a (temporary) setting aside of the state monopoly on force. It is the responsibility of the good citizen and democratic institutions to minimise the extent of any such disturbance. At the same time, a democratic state must ensure that its laws are continually adapted to actual conditions (objective law-making). Normally a state will thus become aware of the consequences of extremes and, as a result, will work to mitigate these. However, as the social coexistence of people develops, this always leads over the long term to greater democracy and greater participation of individuals in government.

The "war of all against all" (Hobbes) is in this situation very unlikely to occur. However, wars involving one state against another and internal civil wars are still feasible and everything possible must be undertaken to prevent such eventualities with all the suffering they cause. In Order to survive, a democracy must put in place and maintain **institutions designed to prevent war and civil war**.

5. Private property

As a democratic state essentially only directly regulates the relationship between its individual citizens, one of the first aspects that needs to be dealt with in such a state is what attitude should be adopted towards things (see Chapter 4). If the **problem of how to distribute assets** was not resolved reasonable, the result would be total extensive conflict for possession of those items which people find attractive in the circumstances and in this situation, it would be impossible to impose laws and a social order (in the sense of positive norms - see Chapter 3).

So people came up with the concept of private property, that assigns those assets to certain people, the owners, who have the exclusive right of exploitation under law. Everyone else, who is not an owner of the asset in question, is excluded from this asset by the **institution of property,** in other words is obligated, without more ado, to not use the asset for their personal benefit.

Because systems used initially to distribute assets were too inept so that the needs of people were left unsatisfied by far, various means of payment (money) were developed in the course of human history; the basic purpose of money is being to provide an easy way of exchanging assets and thus, of course, to facilitate trade. **Money itself** is the abstract, quantifiable property.

The effort required to provide objective legal regulations covering all possible or meaningful uses of any conceivable or existing property would appear to be such that it needed to be assumed that such an attempt would be unworkable in the real world. For this reason also, a stricltly direct definition of private property that differentiated it from other forms of property came into use in the course of the later 20th century.

In the social context, the distribution of assets in the form of private property is known as **capitalism.** In our

21st century, capitalism has become globalised; this means that those who possess considerable private property in one state can move this wealth to any other state – the assignation of the wealth changes only in the course of trade, in the responsibility of business, and to a certain smaller extent because of the need to pay taxes and duties.

Capitalism is anything but perfect and generates its own problems. In 2011, Joseph E. Fargione et al. were able to demonstrate using the so-called *Fargione integral* (https://journals.plos.org/plosone/article?id =10.1371/journal.pone.0020728#aff1) that **over any given time period, existing wealth ultimately becomes concentrated in the hands of a few superrich individuals.** As a result, capitalism – if there is no political intervention – will provide for its own demise. These are issues that every governed state and democracy need to deal with to some extent, although democracy has not yet been established as a form of government everywhere. Potential targets where reform could be initiated would be the institution of private property itself, the rules of trade and wealth related systems of taxation and duties.

6. The generalisation principle

In order to make the connection between the subjective constitution and the will clear, it is necessary to consider the generalisation principle (see Chapter 1 and Chapter 3). The generalisation principle requires the existence of self-awareness; in other words an "ego". This awareness can only be formed after an act of will, that is, after the genesis of a norm before a feel, and experience is thus necessary. **The "ego" resulting from this experience** essentially strives for safety (or "avoidance of risk") and also for control; to put it briefly, one could mean, it strives for status. In the book by Rainer Oesterreich *"Handlungsregulation und Kontrolle" (1981),* control is defined as a tool that can be used to facilitate the achievement of their goals. The ego is thus nothing more than the continuous generator of the sovereign will, if an individual person has the knowledge, that

34

positive and negative norms must be originated by someone (see Chapter 3).

It is, more or less, **human striving for control** that is regulated by Art. 4 of the subjective constitution: "Act only according to that maxim whereby you can at the same time will that it should become a universal law, i.e. a natural principle" (see Chapter 1). This is in effect the same as the **practical imperative, that requires individuals to act in accordance with their knowledge and their will in a controlled fashion under the natural laws.** Art. 4 has been formulated in this way though to demonstrate the interdependence of Arts. 4 and 2 of the subjective constitution.

Art. 2 of the constitution is subjectively necessary for human coexistence, while Art. 4 can become constrained or at least supplanted as a more generalised principle by them more specific ones. Art 2 says: "Act only according to that maxim whereby you can at the same time will that it should become a universal law (i.e. a legal principle)." Now it must be borne in mind that a "law", in the sense of a piece of legislation – as remarked above in connection with the concept of democracy is **generated on the basis of the pool of negative norms of the population of citizens** (see Chapter 4).

It would be possible to have a "law" (piece of legislation) per Art. 2 through which several persons acting in accordance with their own interpretation of Art. 1 and Art. 5 of their subjective constitution would demand something determined from "someone else"; this someone else is able to will meet this demand, finally complies with the nascent law and acts according to it (see Chapter 1). In this connection this law has universal character of applicability, although it might – theoretically - only be expressed by the physical act of the determined person, for it is has been enacted by the will of all people involved.

The transcendency of the generalisation principle may thus be given and although this may be difficult, it is essentially possible, to recognise and to conduct to "laws" which exclusively only evolve on the will of the people. This is presumably what the term **"pure**

respect for the law" as formulated by Immanuel Kant in his generalisation principle means. And it is in this sense that I would like to see the generalisation principle as expressed in Art. 2 of the subjective constitution understood (see Chapter 1). Those who have not considered the generalisation principle in depth, may well understand it as a **principle that requires consideration and care for others**. But only those who act in society in accordance with the generalisation principle will be able to maintain their subjective constitution in this society over the long term.

7. Mutuality: a stepping stone to relationships

A generalisation principle is observed by all rational individuals; however, this is primary understood only in terms of their own, specific principle – in other words, their own concept of objective moral laws (see Chapter 1). At the same time, it is necessary for each person to accept the generalisation principle adopted by the other, involving **mutual recognition of each other's moral code** before the two persons can enter into a viable relationship.

It is not always a matter of course that when two strangers meet, each will be able to respect the generalisation principle of the other – or at least not in full; what is required in addition is **mutual affinity and a certain amount of empathy**.

But not everyone has the necessary empathy – empathy requires that one is willing to become burdened with the sensations, emotions, thoughts, motivations and personality traits of others. Some persons thus take little notice of specific subtleties of communication, such as intonation or selected formulations, that will tell those with empathy a lot about the person they are dealing with.

In accordance with the basic norm, affinity between two individuals involves the one person interpreting the other person as "someone else" (see Chapter 2). **The inevitable result of affinity is always a positive expectation.** A special form of affinity is trust. The person extending trust to the other thus interprets the basic norm in this sense and expects that the "someone else" will not do anything unpleasant to them or harm them. Trust is thus an important prerequisite for the maintenance of personal security (cf. also "negative norms" - see Chapter 3).

Hence, when two people meet, trust must come in first place; this might be followed by increased affinity, empathy and — if the cumulative effect of affinity and empathy is enough — a relationship between the two can come into being.

Depending on the **extent or intensity of the expectations that two individuals in a special relationship have with regard to each other**, the relevance of the corresponding generalisation principles and basic norms will vary in line with the changing significance of the relationship for the constitutions of the subjects (see Chapter 1).

In as far as future events and sensations are the subject of expectations, there is always the **risk that expectations will be disappointed** and that which is expected does not occur in the form demanded or even at all. It is also, that all individuals are quite different by nature, with respect to their ownership of private property, their personal history and so on (see Chapter 5).

The consequence is that in any relationship, certain expectations will be met and others not.

This means that, in order to maintain the moral integrity of its citizens, state institutions need to offer forms of assistance that will appropriately limit and offset the frequently negative impacts of disappointment arising from relationships between persons.

8. Utopia – The kingdom of Me-stock company

Following the example of Immanuel Kant, who, from his *Groundwork of the Metaphysics of Morals*, inferred the generalisation principle, and therefrom the mutuality principle leading to morality and ultimately to a kingdom of ends, I am daring here to draw a conclusion from the subjective constitution that also includes the generalisation principle, leading to the principles of mutuality in relationships and ultimately to a kingdom of Me-stock company (see Chapter 1, Chapter 6 and Chapter 7).

The result of this conclusion, however, is a **utopia, all the more so because it would require not insignificant influences to be suppressed.** In particular, this conclusion requires fading out the question of security, by which I mean that the absolute security of all people in this "kingdom", that is in the

State, would be assumed. Furthermore, it would necessitate imagining the world without any objects, which I will discuss briefly at the end.

Under these conditions, people, as adults, would probably aspire to a sort of **state of monopoly in which they constantly expect more and more positive outcomes from increasingly fewer other people**, whilst at the same time treasuring the stable expectations of others towards themselves as much as possible in order to stay in their favour, thus acting in accordance with the generalisation principle (see Chapter 6). In this, the combination of people's inclination towards each other, which frequently outweighs aversion, and the constitution would, over the life of an individual in a democratic country, lead to each person **being increasingly owned by their fellows in almost the same way as a stock company** and increasingly (even to possible saturation) treated according to the expectations of such "owners"; at the same time, it would also be possible for an inverse ownership to exist.

The **differences between people** in the initial relationships of needs, inclination and perception, including empathy, would have multiple effects on the relationships of expectation and ownership at the end of each contact (see Chapter 7). For example, every sexual act, every commitment or confession, and the extent of any empathy for any human attachment (that is, all institutionalised ownership) would be particularly relevant.

People's ends and aims would be subjected to continuous change due to both cognitive interpretations (especially combinations) and to the concrete applications of all current expectations with respect to the world. **In the end, every subjective constitution would, in conjunction with the others, blend into the background, like a drop of water in the oceans.**

If we assumed that those from whom or from whose ancestors the most was expected in society now have the most money, this utopia could be used to justify the existing distribution of goods (see Chapter 5). Yet

44

this thought contradicts the fiscal sovereignty of the State, which itself has very compelling reasons for being institutionalised. For this reason, as mentioned earlier, the relationship between people and objects, that is the material plane, is of no importance in the kingdom of Me-stock company.

9. Means

When looking at the subjective constitution, it is clear that although Articles 1, 3 and 5 of the basic norm are autonomous and self-evident norms, something important is nonetheless missing. Indeed, there is **no guarantee of enforcement** for these norms, which means there is no prior guarantee that these parts of the constitution will actually be applied and lived out. This is where means have a role to play.

Just as infants have the means to scream when they want to be nursed, adult humans have **a wide variety of options to exert an influence on the target audience of their basic norm for their benefit**. These include bodily functions, formal requests, (potentially) paying money etc. Not all of these options, however, always follow the generalisation principle, especially as the generalisation principle only expresses an "ought", whereas some options are actually very damaging to humanity, as for instance, the frequent and sudden use of violence (see Chapter 6).

Nevertheless, a person needs to be able to apply their own basic norm to their life, which implies the occasional enforcement of the basic norm; here, however, the "ought" tends to be inverted, especially as **the subject of the "ought" can only enforce the basic norm through their own means**. This is why democracy provides many objective laws that require a target audience, composed of subjects with certain means, to safeguard a specific interest in the event of other constraints (see Chapter 4). Objective legislation generally restricts itself to prescribing a framework in which those subject to the law can conclude contracts that enable at least a unilateral enforcement of the basic norm.

In the "kingdom of Me-stock company" utopia, **means would generally have to be distributed according to the need** (see Chapter 8). In other words, every person would must dispose of sufficient resources to enforce their own basic norm. To this extent, a material plane can in fact be retrospectively inserted into the utopia, even though "means" refers to possible action rather than possessions. As it represents prosperity, this should be a social aim, yet in practice, complete prosperity can barely be achieved.

The question whether a strong will is sufficient to enforce one's basic norm can here be answered in the negative: The target audience of the basic norm, whether it be a woman, an object or a man, continues to exercise its own will and will follow it even when dealing with the norms of others (see Chapter 3). **The means used by another must therefore carry the appropriate appeal to move the audience to actually comply with the norm.**

10. The pursuit of happiness

The U.S. American Declaration of Independence (https://en.wikipedia.org/wiki/United_States_Declaration_of_Independence) lists the **pursuit of happiness as an unalienable human right.** Without seeking to define an objective meaning of happiness, I do interpret happiness, by the way, as a subjective elation similar to euphoria, although based on more objective factors than the latter.

As, on the basis of the subjective constitution, we have accepted the extreme points of the generalisation principle and the basic norm, the **happiness pursued must be found within these two extremes** (see Chapter 1). The pursuit of happiness is thus susceptible to subjective interpretation. In other words: **The key to happiness lies in self-awareness** and the subjective constitution makes a decisive contribution to this.

Therefore, when pursuing happiness, we must interpret the extremes according to the state of the art in such a way as to constitute the facts that promise happiness, among other things, and maybe even bring them about by our own means (see Chapter 9). For more background on this interpretation, please consult the rich literature on the generalisation principle, including texts by Immanuel Kant and responses to him. With regards to the basic norm, the most helpful tools are **scientific interpretation methods** (such as those developed in Sections 6 and following of the General Civil Code developed in Austrian law), as well as memory: indeed, a subject's recollections are essential for interpreting the basic norm according to the theory of originalism. The practical interpretations of fellow human beings can also help understand the concepts of constitution and happiness, such as these remarks. Knowledge and happiness are not mutually exclusive. Nor does the happiness of a subject mean that they are passive. On the contrary, as the subjective constitution already indicates, **being happy is always a dynamic process**, although the constitution does create a meaningful framework in which personal happiness can be pursued. **Awareness of their subjective constitution therefore increases each person's chance of happiness.**

However, **no one has a claim to happiness** and, as already described in the article on the kingdom of Me-stock company, people aspire towards a state of monopoly in exchange relationships (see Chapter 8). This raises the question of whether and to what extent such monopolies can cause a lack of supply of happiness for other people (and therefore to worries) or other significant problems?

Such considerations do not however impede the clear improvement that the subjective constitution represents for all interested parties, and for democracy (see Chapter 4). Even the latter ultimately has the task of solving widespread social worries. My suggestion for an individual's process would therefore be, despite a happy experience, to always remember that someone or something else is to be put before oneself. It is **humility that transforms experienced happiness into the healthy happiness** that remains worth striving for.

11. Conflict

From the fact that all people have basic norms in their subjective constitution and that **humans are the dominant lifeform on Earth**, it follows that the environment is disputed between people (see Chapter 1). This means that some goods and raw materials are "scarce" etc. Mankind is dependent upon many such goods for its well-being and development.

In this context, the generalisation principle requests that, insofar as our own needs are largely met, we **consider the needs of other people as well**, and in particular, provide actively for any basic needs they are still lacking (see Chapter 6). (The fact that millions of people are still victims of starvation is therefore greatly to the shame of mankind.)

However, the **scarcity of goods**, especially of high value goods, essentially leads to the following outcome: When two or more people want something specific, such as owning an object as private property that ultimately only one person, or just not everyone, can have, **a conflict follows** (see Chapter 3 and Chapter 5). Insofar as the conflicting parties do not think in the way promoted by the subjective constitution or, more concretely, by the generalisation principle – whether because they need to meet their own basic needs or because the conflicting parties are lacking in sense – the conflict is likely to escalate to a violent fight.

The state theorist Thomas Hobbes, in his main work *The Leviathan, Chapter XIII,* justified the **necessity of a public state** due to human nature. According to him, there are *"three principal causes of quarrel. First, competition; secondly, diffidence; thirdly, glory."* In addition: *"Hereby it is manifest that during the time men live without a common power to keep them all in awe, they are in that condition which is called war; and such a war as is of every man against every man."* This argument is striking, especially as, in such a situation of war of every man against every man, it is impossible to assume that one's reasons are better than another's without the existence of an overarching framework. An orderly resolution of disputes, or **"legal peace", is therefore an important purpose** of any state.

Indeed, insofar as a disputing party **is able to recognise the primacy of the law** under which the dispute can be resolved peacefully, it further enables them to identify how to behave reasonably in such situations. They can also identify how to satisfy the need in question. The overarching law must not discriminate subjectively, as it is precisely **the grounds for its decisions that give meaning to cohesion**.

Furthermore, almost every conflict that does not revolve around basic survival is subject to an overarching principle. The growing experience of institutional judicial authorities enables the cohesion of society to be seen as increasingly stable (see Chapter 4). Against the backdrop of an increasingly globalised world and broadening cosmopolitan world views, this is also a growing area of tension between national states.

The expediency of avoiding conflict and resolving disputes must not obscure the fact **that every conflict also offers opportunities**. In particular when the consequences of a conflict are not too destructive, such disputes should actually be allowed to be open-ended. This enabled the conflicting parties to find motivation for particular objectives and possibly change for the good and even develop further. Where would humanity be today without its conflicts?

12. On the process of subjective law-making

For this analysis, we must assume that the two (or five) poles of the subjective constitution already existed prior to initial law-making – that is, the **constitutional framework of a person was already a hereditary foundation**, before they were ever capable, as a subject, to create their own subjective law (see Chapter 1).

The first stage, that is the act of (original) stimulation from outside, from the environment, corresponds to the subject's basic norm, thus activating the basic norm (for the first time - see also Chapter 2). In some not fully definable way, the **activation of the basic norm** injects energy into the subject's inner being. Energy should be understood as the potential to do one's work. The energy in the subject is then altered subjectively and thus **an initially abstract subjective**

"law" develops in the subject's inner being, that has form but no specific content.

This blank law can even sometimes express itself, such as through a subject's uncontrolled movements. However, once the abstract law has been created, the next step essentially sees the deployment of **the subject's sensory perception**, which experiences meaningful information through the outside world and incorporates this into the subjective law, thus giving the law some content, in this case a (subjective) truth.

From time to time, sovereign will arises from subjective truth (see Chapter 3). Such will best corresponds to the generalisation principle **when the subjective truth from which it has arisen resembles the "general law" of the generalisation principle**; however, insofar as this feature is an ideal concept, the sovereign will can, in reality, only correspond approximately to the generalisation principle.

This means that for some readers, the **idea of a world view** may be more relevant or appropriate than that of subjective truth. It is essential to remember, however, that it must at least correspond to the subjective law, as well as more or less to the general law of the generalisation principle. Indeed, the **concept of law expresses that (human) relationships are regulated in a binding manner.**

The subject will put their subjective truth into effect in the outside world and will therefore **behave in a subjectively moral manner.** In this, the closer the concept of subjective law comes to the general law of the generalisation principle, the more inspiring and authoritative the law becomes for external third parties or for the environment; however, it is impossible to push the boundaries of our own subjective perception at will to all extend, in order to qualify our subjective truth.

Generally, significant life experience is needed to develop our subjective truth. And thus we come full circle: Once a subject has acted more or less morally according to their will, they live through certain experiences that infiltrate the subjective "law" through sensory perception (or through the basic norm) and cause the subjective truth to evolve until the time comes again for the will to rise up and act.

It is essential for the intelligence to structure its concept of law – or any similar applicable subjective concept. Essentially, the concept of law expresses the regulation of (human) relationships. However, as described in the subjective constitution, a hierarchy of laws can be assumed etc. (see Chapter 1). Even **sex can be understood, under certain conditions, as a "law"**, one dealing with reproduction or health, for example.

13. Equality

A general definition of "equal" is that which does not differ in a given feature, whilst abstracting all other features and any difference thereby created. But when are people equal? What is **"equality before the law"**?

The objective constitutions of all democratically organised states include legislation on equality, that is a **ban on subjective discrimination** towards their citizens, which prohibits state discrimination according to e.g. sex, age, origin, language, race, religion, class, disability etc. (see Chapter 4). However, these do not note explicitly what specific features citizens do not (should not) differ in.

Because we are dealing with democracies, the following attribute seems clear, in any case: **Citizens are equal in that they will the objective law of their homeland.** This conclusion is implicit legal fiction in that the "will" does not have to be empirically proven to exist in individual cases, such as when a criminal is being trialed. However, by and large, the fiction that all citizens will the objective law must be sustained, or the democracy in question would lose its **legitimacy** and founder.

This is why equality before the law is such an important principle of democracy. A democratic state should only act against the equality of its citizens if this would irrefutably be to their greatest advantage and can be convincingly argued and justified, at which point divisions in society would need to be avoided!

The **concept of equality** is also very interesting with regard to the subject and their subjective constitution, in particular in the two following aspects (see Chapter 1):

-        Where a subject is the equal of a third party, that is **the subject wills the same thing as the other person**, this could lead to a conflict in the event of a given scarcity or, insofar as there is no scarcity, the two equal persons always have the option of acting according to the generalisation principle (see Chapter

11). In the latter case, i.e. when two people are agreed about willing the same thing, we sometimes talk of **love**. If the lovers are in a relationship and their love is long-lasting, this gives the lovers' morality — which is in line with their common desire — an additional impulse (see Chapter 7).

- If a subject has to judge **whether two people or objects external to themselves are equal**, they will make this assessment using their subjective truth and their experience (see Chapter 12). Assuming they do not simply align with social convention, they will have to determine **what feature is the decisive factor for equality or inequality**. Ultimately, this judgement can involve some intense soul-searching on the part of the subject for, as the proverb says, "the devil is in the detail" and from an existential point of view, no two appearances are fully identical. The more correct the subject's subjective truth, the more **equitable** their judgement will turn out to be.

Why does the subjective constitution, specifically the basic norm, **on closer inspection** distinguish between male and female, and objects? Because, although in my personal experience, the thought process of each sex is equally valid, **the priorities in the thoughts of each** have basic opposing structures, presumably due to physiological differences.

We normally believe that objects do not think. However, insofar as they belong to the private property of someone other than the subject, we can, under certain conditions and in accordance with the basic norm, associate objects directly with the person in question; this means that **we might see objects in the same way as we see their owner** (see Chapter 5). What we actually consider objects are therefore those that are common property and that form the subject's own private property. In principle, this deals with every form of energy that can be transmitted from the object to the subject, such as the bread eaten for supper. For the basic norm to be effective, it is actually enough for **an object to "strike the senses"**.

Why would the generalisation principle, when considering the subjective constitution more closely, distinguish between legal laws and natural laws (see Chapter 1)? Because this is first and foremost a question of **perspective**. In real life, people are surrounded by a magnetic field and electromagnetic tensions are processed in their brains. However, this last phenomenon can only be observed from outside.

Yet external observation is subordinate, especially when it comes to morality. Indeed, **moral action always has inner, tangible added value for the subject**. Whereas the imperative to "act only according to that maxim whereby you can at the same time will that it should become a universal law (as a natural law)" is morally less important and fundamentally only demands the subject to act controlled.

14. Self-esteem

We know from the section on the subjective constitution that the generalisation principle and the basic norm represent extremes between which the subjective constitution is found (see Chapter 1). We know from the section on the process of subjective law-making that **a subjective "law" is found in the inner being**, first as an abstract, then primarily as a structured concept (see Chapter 12). The subjective constitution requires the subject to have basic self-esteem.

This self-esteem could be expressed in how we treasure the relevance of the laws we apply and on the basis of which we can register concrete successes. Or it could be expressed in how we treasure the binding character of our laws, especially when we occasionally receive compliments from other people. Or by how we treasure the clout of our laws when overcoming given obstacles. But no matter how our self-appreciation is expressed (as this depends greatly on the individual quality of structured subjective law), the **most important question remains from what and to what total extent the self-esteem exists.**

People who have too little self-esteem are often desperate and depressed. We can remedy this by aligning ourselves with the basic norm in a positive sense: **Look for specific pleasant influences or specific pleasant sensations** and then seek to repeat these experiences at regular intervals according to the basic norm. This forced application of the basic norm stimulates and increases self-esteem. At the same time, I must highlight the problematic risk of addiction to some seemingly pleasant experiences, especially drugs!

People who have too much self-esteem are often selfish and found intolerable by other people. We can remedy this by aligning ourselves with the generalisation principle, in that we examine everything we intend to do and consider if the relevant maxim of the will can be presented as a general law. Actually, by making this examination regularly for all possible determinants of action, **we will develop more and more selfless maxims of the will that come closer and closer to a general will and a general law.** If we end up almost sacrificing ourselves to fulfil a general law, we can surely orient our inner selves more towards our basic norm in order to feel more self-esteem.

In this way, every subject empowers their subjective constitution to personally regulate their well-being, which is linked with self-esteem, and thus to personally accentuate their own constitution. A rational subject will exercise this ability with planning their pursuit of happiness so that they always feel happy, to a greater or lesser balanced extent, in being prepared for the unexpected (see Chapter 10). In the utopic case of the kingdom of Me-stock company, this would be an important focus for everyone (see Chapter 8).

15. The theory of originalism

In the chapter on the subjective constitution, I mentioned that the norms of a subjective constitution, just like objective constitutional norms, are essentially to be interpreted according to the theory of originalism. I will discuss this stipulation here.

In the chapter on subjective law-making, we assumed that the **constitutional framework was originally a hereditary foundation** (see Chapter 12). This assumption is the only possible option, in view of the intersubjectivity found on all sides, the self-evident character of both, the generalisation principle and the basic norm: Every single person must have inherited their subjective constitution. This conclusion implies that the constitutional norms of the subjective constitution must be comprehended *a priori*; in fact, they determine our life from the very start.

However, it is possible **to draw a personal benefit from an active awareness of our subjective constitution**: It allows us to plan and control our lives much more effectively, to experience emotions more consciously and to find personal happiness more easily. If someone enters a conflict in full awareness of their subjective constitution, this awareness will work itself out to their material or immaterial advantage: Indeed, the stable foundation of the subjective constitution is a very assertive friend, especially as it is unassailable **as the fundamental link between the subject's morality and hope** (see Chapter 11). Thus, a subject's constitutional norms are particularly useful because of their unique rigidity.

If we want an action or experience to become a subjective habit, we call upon the will (see Chapter 3). When the relevant will is present, i.e. the **action or experience is wilfully perceived to be pleasant**, our mind will subjectively create a corresponding habit norm based on the will. According to the theory of originalism, all the individual circumstances that existed at the time of the action or experience are drawn upon to create such a norm. In a subject's everyday life, however, uncountable habits occur that have not been created according to the concept of originalism. **Nevertheless, the more important a habit is for the subject's life, the more rigid its determining norm will essentially be.**

It is clear for all these reasons that the subjective constitution must be interpreted just as it had been inherited, that is according to the theory of originalism (see Chapter 1). In my opinion, this means, in principle, that the existing subjective constitution embodies the inherited foundation of enlightened humanity in every human subject. The **concept of the "dignity of man"** could not be better outlined.

16. The system of hope

I am certain that some readers derived this directly from the phrase "Someone else ought to feed me" mentioned at the beginning: the basic norm of every mammal in its essence incorporates nothing less than **the most general principle of hope conceivable** (see Chapter 2). A German proverb claims that hope is the last thing to die — I believe in any case that hope, in the form of the basic norm, is also the first thing in the life of any mammal. The earlier remarks therefore form part of the process of subjective law-making (see Chapter 12). But how is hope (further) developed during life?

Understanding the original principle of hope, or basic norm, is of "eternal" value for, as soon as this principle is completely extinguished in the spirit of a subject, that subject would be doomed to die. But with hope, we don't need to remain at the level of the basic norm; rather, it is essential for a healthy life to create and constantly have constant, special, specific and targeted hopes. **In any case, specific hopes are indispensable to produce pleasant experiences.** Hopes can be created unconsciously or consciously.

The main problem in creating a specific hope is the fact that **there is only a given probability that the hoped-for outcome** will occur, and it is often dependent upon means (see Chapter 9). And this despite the fact that the subject is disposed towards the hoped-for outcome, which means that if the outcome does not occur, they will suffer from the lack. Thankfully, society, or the people to whom the subject relates in society, can help to fulfil unfulfilled hopes or to turn them into something that can be fulfilled and ultimately to eradicate unmet needs (or lacks - see Chapter 7). This means that almost every person in an affluent society, in particular the middle-aged, can continuously fulfil relatively specific or targeted hopes and wishes.

In order to **become aware of the unconscious hopes that involuntarily influence a subject**, I highly recommend the psychotherapeutic approach of Richard C. Schwartz in *Internal Family Systems Therapy*, for example. This basically assumes that the mind (or spirit) is made up of inner parts with which we can communicate respectfully. Important sovereignty grows from the awareness of our own hopes, dreams and wishes, for a subject's willpower only exists in awareness (see Chapter 3).

Insofar as we consciously control our hopes, I believe that it is **generally advantageous to have many weaker hopes rather than fewer strong ones**. On the one hand, this reduces the risk of a major disappointment to our hopes; after all, disappointments are an important part of life. On the other hand, it means we see the people and things to which we pin our hopes in a different and brighter light: These people and things already have a subjectively pleasant impact on the subject, even when they possibly deceive in that they are in the process of fulfilling a particular hope. This attribute makes it a lot easier to transform a hope and to eradicate a lack.

74

For this reason, from the viewpoint of a pleasant and healthy sensation, it is a **meaningful priority to "believe in the good in people"**. This logic could be answered in some circumstances by a cool and calculating — but probably less healthy — principled position in accordance with the generalisation principle which said that we should basically not deceive ourselves for real (see Chapter 6).

17. Induction — Deduction

One of the benefits of the subjective constitution is to demonstrate reason and organise things more consciously. The induction and deduction processes describe clearly and in detail the type of movements that the subjective constitution makes towards the generalisation principle or towards the basic norm. When desired, **induction and deduction can express the methods** of the mental or even — with the appropriate body sensation of a subject — nervous moves through to the relevant conclusion.

Deduction derives a conclusion for the inner self from the external everything (community) and indirectly targets the absorption of energy. Deduction thus activates the basic norm or a more special hope that builds on it (see The system of hope - Chapter 16). When a hope is fulfilled by a deductive conclusion, energy is absorbed to the same degree as the internal satisfaction. Self-esteem grows at the same time, depending on the measure of subjective pleasure at the fulfilment (see Chapter 14). Depending on the specific deductive conclusion, an empirical value is created that flows into the subjective law along with the energy absorbed and there modifies the truth; thus law is subjectively created (see Chapter 12).

Induction derives a conclusion for the general everything (community) from existing subjective law and is indirectly targeted at spreading information. Induction thus examines the equality of the relevant subjective law with a projected law that could apply to the general everything (community) in relation to the specific information that needs to be disseminated (see Chapter 13). If this equality essentially exists and (more or less) corresponds to the generalisation principle, an inductive conclusion is drawn (see Chapter 6). This basically means that an action will follow to disseminate the information in question in the form of a law. Self-esteem decreases slightly in proportion to the loss of the exclusive character of the objectively disseminated information for the acting subject (see Chapter 14). Induction always needs energy and appropriate information gleaned from the subjective constitution and realises the subject's inner self in the outside environment.

Both processes are vital and constantly complement each other; in my opinion, they cannot be conceptually restricted to a purely philosophical cognitive process, but rather should also be applied to nervous impulses, for example, according to a further understanding of the backdrop of the subjective constitution. After all, induction is much talked about in the electromagnetic field and we might also see induction and deduction as **electromagnetic processes** in humans.

18. Legal positivism

These days, there are legal philosophy theories about objective laws according to which law comes from human nature: these are natural law theories as opposed to what is known as legal positivism. Simply put, legal positivism emphasizes the priority of the **form of the law as its distinguishing feature**: Any content, as long as it is issued in the appropriate formal process can, according to legal positivism, essentially become an authoritative law.

Hans Kelsen, arguably the most important proponent of legal positivism of the 20th century, states in his main work Pure Theory of Law, Chapter V, 35, a) The Constitution, p. 228: "The legal order is not a system of coordinated norms of equal level, but a hierarchy of different levels of legal norms. Its unity is brought about by the connection that results from the fact that **the validity of the norm, created according to another norm, rests on that other norm, whose**

creation, in turn, is determined by a third one." There is therefore a regression which, according to Kelsen, results in a 'basic norm' (whereby this 'basic norm' does not have the same meaning as that in the subjective constitution, but rather should be understood as the "will for a legal system" implemented by citizens, as mentioned in the section on equality - see Chapter 1 and Chapter 13).

However, just a few pages earlier, in the section specified as 34, i) Basic norm theory and natural law theory, p. 224, Kelsen explains his 'basic norm': "According to the Pure Theory of Law, as a positivistic legal theory, no positive legal order can be regarded as not conforming with its 'basic norm' and hence as not valid. **The content of a positive legal order is entirely independent from its 'basic norm'.** For ─ the point must be stressed ─ only the validity, not the content of a legal order can be derived from the 'basic norm'." [Kelsen's 'basic norm' has been emphasised with speech marks for the purposes of better conceptual differentiation.]

In contrast to such arbitrariness of the content of objective law, natural law proponents, such as Gustav Radbruch or John Rawls, in the 20th century, assert that **law should serve justice**. Justice is essentially understood as the commandment to treat equal things equally and what is not equal differently (cf. Equality - see Chapter 13).

The decisive problem with legal positivism is, as natural law proponents argue, that its arbitrariness legitimises unjust totalitarian systems, such as the Nazi Reich. The main problem with natural law theory, on the other hand, is the difficulty — or even impossibility — of objectivising justice, as this is almost always dependent upon the observer's own point of view.

This is why Western democracies **currently apply a "mixed system"** as the basis for objective law: On the one hand, objective law applies because it has been issued as such in a formal constitution; on the other hand, objective law should serve justice. The direct consequence of this mixed system is that **trained lawyers interpret objective law as they want: lawyers who practise private law predominantly treat the content of the law as just, whilst those who practise public law predominantly treat it as having come about formally.** In view of history, this consequence should on no account be rejected. Nevertheless, I believe that future paths should, as far as possible, lead towards an increasingly institutional separation of powers (see Democracy - Chapter 4) in order to create fairer laws under very solemn requirements.

19. Is — Ought

According to the famous **"Hume's law"**, named after the philosopher David Hume, any conclusion about what ought to be that is drawn from what is, is illogical. Even Hans Kelsen, the prominent proponent of legal positivism, for example, presented a strict division between "is" and "ought" in his work *Pure Theory of Law* (see Chapter 18). This basic relationship of "is" and "ought" should be studied, in particular with regard to the subjective constitution, which is determined by norms, or "ought" statements, that are derived from an actual "is", i.e. human life (see Chapter 1).

In the sections discussing the basic norm and the sovereign will, I simply described how **experience is the basis for the temporal shift of a norm before the corresponding sensation** (see Chapter 2 and Chapter 3). Georg Jellinek, *General Theory of State, Book 2, Chapter 11,* p. 338, justifies his conclusion of what ought to be from what is as follows: *"It would be* entirely wrong to locate the **normative power of the factual** in its conscious or unconscious reasonableness. *The factual can be rationalised at a later date, but its normative quality lies in the feature of our nature, which is not derivable further, in virtue of which the already Practiced is physiologically and psychologically much easier reproduced than the New.*"

In my opinion, both Jellinek and Kelsen have exposed important pieces of the puzzle. Nevertheless, I believe that an "ought" cannot follow from a plain reproduction of "the already Practiced" as suggested by Jellinek. Rather, an **anticipation of corresponding future events is also required.** However, this anticipation can only occur if the experience that is being reproduced provides the subject with an **impulsive excess of energy** such that the subject can only convert into a projection (the "ought"). Thus, the transition from "is" to "ought" is a similar process as a deduction with (immediately subsequent) induction (see Chapter 17). Essentially, this anticipates a part

84

of the subjective truth, which can also involve **some genetic information** (see Chapter 12). In particular, where information is the object of the anticipatory projection, the blank form of the relevant norm will continue to exist. Now, the subject can pour their excess of energy into the future-orientated new form and live out and experience the norm they have just created, as well as examine it in the light of later experience and adapt it.

Hume and Kelsen have both however correctly argued **that in most cases, an "ought" conclusion based on an "is" is a fallacy**: Information anticipated from a practical exercise is the product of an impulsive induction and is therefore uncontrolled to a relatively high degree or dependent upon chance. Consequently, "ought" conclusions based on "is" statements should generally be avoided. This also means that Kelsen's legal positivism, with its emphasis on the legal form and its derivation of "oughts" almost exclusively from other "oughts", represents an entirely appropriate legal philosophy for public order and (legal) security in a state (see Chapter 18). Obviously, this only applies insofar as no totalitarianism arises, which would inevitably lead to war.

The reverse conclusion, from an "ought" to an "is", is more plausible and simpler to argue insofar as it is already conceptually given: Indeed, **"ought" expresses an imperative**, that is a compulsive piece of information. Anyone confronted with it can draw a more or less corresponding "is" statement from it, whereby the compulsion essentially fulfils its purpose and the norm gains in significance, or oppose it with a contradictory "is" statement, which could, in extreme cases, lead to conflict (see Chapter 11). In particular, as the intensity of the compulsion (cf. basic norm - Chapter 2) or tolerance vis-à-vis the compulsion can vary, only statements of probability can be made *ex ante*.

20. Fear

Fear is the antithesis of hope and should therefore be discussed (see Chapter 16). Fear is the basic principle of an unpleasant sensation that generally happens, although less frequently than hope (see Chapter 3). Summing up fear in an abstract formula as for the basic norm would not achieve any original benefit due to the **intractable nature of fear**. In contrast, such a form of fear would artificially move or project you into a type of "cage". I will therefore refrain from formulating a "basic norm of fear".

Experienced fear basically has no value for the subject in terms of causing a positive effect, rather it destroys control, **causes chaotic reflexes, contractions and constraints** (see Chapter 6). When of average intensity, fear strongly compels the subject to avoid sensing it again. In high intensity, fear can lead to panic, which can unleash completely unpredictable behaviour. The experience of extremely strong fear can leave the subject with psychological disorders. For this reason, although fear is still very important for humans, it is **not a component or element** of the subjective constitution (see Chapter 1).

Nevertheless, fear is important and meaningful for humans insofar as, when experienced in the right measure, it leads to the creation of negative norms that can **empower the subject** (see Chapter 3). Thus, even subjective laws that are necessary for survival could require experiencing specific fears (see Chapter 12). Younger people in particular should therefore also add to their experience "more thrilling" activities that are linked to a little fear as long as the risks of such activities can be calculated.

Engagement with **occurrences that make them fearful** can either benefit a subject in that it enables them to develop their norms particularly well, or injure them in that it removes options because of the loss of control. In conflicts in particular, one participant could feel fear before another, for instance (see Chapter 11). Of crucial importance when engaging with specific, fear-provoking occurrences is the degree of self-esteem that the subject applies (see Chapter 14). **With enough self-esteem and the power of hope** embodied in the basic norm, certain fears can generally be overcome. To eradicate chronic fear, a conscious and controlled confrontation with specific fear-inducing situations could be helpful.

Although fear is in principle a negative thing, **no one should go through life without any fear at all**. Some smaller fears in particular, which can be controlled with one's own self-esteem, offer the subject practical opportunities or reduce practical risks. Thanks to the interplay of fear and hope that this opens up, short-term success can sometimes be achieved which would have remained unachievable without **the agitation and sensitisation caused by fear**. Ultimately, however, it is important for hope to win.

Heinz Bude, in his work *Society of Fear*, has studied, described and summarised some of the current sociological phenomena of fear. I would recommend *Society of Fear* for anyone wanting to delve deeper into this topic.

21. Empathy

Empathy has already been presented as a skill in other chapters, such as the one on interpersonal relationships (see Chapter 7). However, empathy deserves a more detailed examination, especially as it represents a particularly valuable skill. **Everyone can learn empathy to a given degree.** And everyone should be able to call up a little of it vis-à-vis another person – at least, this would be a widespread claim linked to the generalisation principle (cf. what is known as the "Formula of the End" of the categorical imperative – or see Chapter 6).

The first thing that is important for a subject's empathy is sharp senses, as a basic **highly attentive observation** of all other people, or at least of all the people the subject wants to be empathetic towards, is required. The second requirement for empathy is the inductive imagined scenario of **the subject themselves being in the place of the other person** (see Chapter 17). This imagined scenario does not need to be at all comprehensive or perfect to start with. Rather, an initial time-limited projection is enough, provided that accurate observation is maintained. The third requirement for empathy is the deductive conclusion that follows from the combination of sensory observation and the imagined perspective: What does the person need now (see Chapter 17)?

Increasing experience of empathy towards a particular person will enable a subject to answer more and more far-reaching questions about the feelings, emotions, thoughts, motives and personality features of the person. For example: How will the person seek to achieve their current goals? How will the person feel when they obtain certain information? etc.

However, empathy requires affection and energy. The more pronounced the empathy, the more affection is needed to maintain it. **The degree of empathy a subject can feel is therefore naturally limited.** If empathy towards to a given person requires too much energy that is not offset by the offer of mutual empathy, this can often be grounds for ending the interpersonal relationship with that person (see Chapter 7).

In addition, persons (strangers) who do not believe in the good in people can feel fear and distrust towards subjects who are watching them closely (see Chapter 16 and Chapter 20). Indeed, **when people nurture bad intentions towards others**, there is an additional risk that they will use the knowledge they have gained about such others for their own ends. Yet, empathy cannot develop or grow without closely observing the people in question.

As a subject grows older, if they have already collected some experiences of empathy towards other people, they **will increasingly generalise their experiences**; this means, for instance, that they will draw inductive conclusions about the general behavioural principles that are behind the specific behaviour of several people (as well as test these conclusions). The subjective truth is thus always increasingly polished (see Chapter 12). People calling

93

forth – stronger – empathy will become rarer.

Where there is a lack of empathy or if the truth suggests incorrect conclusions, this often leads to misunderstandings. In this case, the subject assumes purposes that the person in question does not have at all. Misunderstandings reduce the self-esteem of the participants and are often the cause of conflict (see Chapter 11 and Chapter 14).

22. Determinism

Whether consciously or subconsciously, every person pursues goals in their life. I have already explained in detail in relation to the sovereign will how the **subject's goal is generally always a sensation** (see Chapter 3). However, it might not always be comprehended as such, as some sensations occur on a purely transcendent level, outside of consciousness.

The sensations a subject hopes for can be linked to a particular external process or several external processes etc. Often, the sensations that are the goal are ultimately **provided by the subject's sensory perception**. It can sometimes happen that a given goal is only recognised as such when the corresponding sensation is experienced.

I believe that the goals that a subject achieves in their life are always determined in advance. **Ultimately, nothing happens by chance.** Nevertheless, it depends on all the individual decisions and efforts of every subject. For the will is sovereign and only by unfolding it in a way we perceive to be free, can anything be understood to be "achieved".

The subject's will decides what hopes the subject takes on board (see Chapter 16). The same will chooses from its means how to achieve its goals and essentially controls all its actions to this end (see Chapter 9). Should these functions of the will be summarised as the "pursuit of happiness" (see Chapter 10)? Possibly. However, the **question of success** is always a causality between cause and effect.

The consequence of this point of view is that every **failure basically offers the opportunity to understand its grounds** and so learn something useful for our life. Thus, every opportunity is prescribed in principle. On the other hand, it is never advisable to rely upon an "invisible hand" or similar, rather **every thought that is thought and every authentic movement is an important part of the puzzle** on which humanity has been working since its beginnings. Religion might be a part of the solution for every person or even an ultimate wholesum, hiding behind everything we recognise. Insofar as is presented here, however, religion — Pascal's wager notwithstanding — is not necessarily a component of a subjective truth (see Chapter 12). The **subjective truth is always the mainstay of sensitivities** in the context of the subjective constitution and continually wants to disentangle itself, encouraged by the conscious or subconscious pursuit of subjective goals (see Chapter 1). By and large, it does this just as if it was decreed by corresponding causes.

Through the disentanglement or clarification of their subjective truth, every person gains insights into both, themselves and the environment, although the subject is generally only ever aware of one of the two aspects. Humanity as a whole would gain if the exchange of **intersubjective transparent truths** was always quick, easy and safe. However, even these questions relate to success and are therefore already determined at the time of their pertinence.

23. Human rights

The sections on private property and on the pursuit of happiness have already broached two special human rights (see Chapter 5 and Chapter 10). Some also see equality before the law as a human right, however, human rights are only usually recognised in democracies (see Chapter 4 and Chapter 13).

Human rights are outflows of natural law and therefore, on a theoretical level, they contradict legal positivism (see Chapter 18). According to the theory of originalism, the establishment of human rights, in particular with regard to the United Nations' Universal Declaration of Human Rights and the European Convention on Human Rights, represents the **reaction of humanity to the atrocities before and during World War II** (see Chapter 15).

Insofar as human rights are upheld in a state, these hold an (objective) constitutional rank, which is why we also talk of **constitutional rights**. Based on the constitution, human rights theoretically prevail in the application of law in every case. In themselves, constitutional rights mean that these rights should almost always be respected, however, the subjective recognition of natural rights is sometimes too difficult, which is why human rights can be violated.

Practice and the observation of human rights when applying the law can favour subjective empathy (see Chapter 21). This practice also gives birth to an objective **concept of proportionality** with which the highest legal jurisdiction determines individual human rights in consideration of the democratic benchmarks of relevance, scope and/or clout in order to make such natural laws or corresponding minimum standards more recognisable in the practical application of law.

The human rights system is the **best system worldwide for the benefit of mankind** and yet it is constantly under threat. The main reason for such instability of human rights is, I believe, a tolerated disproportion of private property: Indeed, some subjects already hold so many rare means and naturally always want more, so that over time, it becomes increasingly hard for the majority of humankind to meet their needs (see Chapter 5 and Chapter 9). This **scarcity of means** artificially leads to more conflict between people and, should a state of emergency arise for any reason, fewer and fewer people have the option of effectively relieving this state of emergency (see Chapter 11).

Private property, which is so essential for the subjective constitution in small and medium measures, is, when of a disproportionate degree, an extreme risk to the peace and well-being of whole peoples and countries, **due to its exclusive nature** (see Chapter 1). However, as long as no general illuminating limits to private property can be shown or discovered and thus objective constitutional norms cannot be justified, in order to restrict the extent of subjective means in a meaningful framework, in extreme inequalities any reasonable subject of a democracy must soon continually call on those superrich individual subjects to please place their disproportionate private property for the utility of the state.

The subjective constitution gives the subject **a superordinate level of worth** when it comes to human rights. We know the paths that constitute a threat to human rights, even to those of the subject themselves, and we can exercise our sovereign will to deflect the greater evil (see Chapter 3). Even if the outcome of the conflict is already determined in advance (see Chapter 22).

24. Sustainability

Even when aware of our subjective constitution, it is often appropriate to see **life as a type of metabolic process in a cycle** (see Chapter 1). The process of subjective law-making can also be described in this way (see Chapter 12). A cycle is also used when dealing with the concept of sustainability: Sustainability corresponds to an **obligation to preserve and protect the cycle of nature** in order to maintain the existing environmental conditions (for descendants), an obligation derived from the generalisation principle (see Chapter 6).

The principle of sustainability thus essentially means ensuring, as a first step, **that all that people take from nature and everything they give to nature** is harmless for nature and its cycle. In a second step, what is taken and given should be adjusted to a harmless quantity. Sustainability exists insofar as the taking and giving are really harmless, i.e. nature essentially continues unchanged.

The external cycle of nature is thus abstractly the counterpart to the internal cycle of subjective law-making. This cycle can only function and continue if the subject withdraws energy from the environment from time to time. The **realisation of full sustainability in principle must therefore fail due to the nature of humans** for whose very survival specific sensitive processes are indispensable.

Reasonably, therefore, sustainability can only mean that, by and large, we avoid unnecessary harm to the cycle of nature. However, to find the right objective extent here seems to me ultimately to be almost more difficult than to exercise objective justice (see Chapter 13). For this reason, a democracy must commit itself as a whole to this issue (see Chapter 4).

Even if it seems extremely important to maintain the environment or habitat for the generations to come, **change over time is also a basic principle of nature and its life**. Particularly because mankind must, due to its natural striving for control, always make it a goal to control and rule over its environment, there exists a **principle of the primacy of humanity**, including maintaining and developing the human race, over such sustainability (see Chapter 6).

Finally, nature itself is repeatedly capable of regenerating what has been harmed, adapting what exists to new conditions or even developing something completely new. Those who **fight for sustainability often have the most comprehensive and practical knowledge** of how far the self-healing powers of nature (can) actually reach. Because the possibility and even the **risk of extreme damage to the environment have recently** and unfortunately increased significantly, sustainability is becoming an increasingly important political issue. In the 21st century therefore, we need each activity to be considered in proportion to the principle of sustainability.